COME *to the* MOUNTAIN

---

*Learning to Live
Out of a Full Heart*

DEBORAH STRICKLIN

Come to the Mountain

by Deborah Rae Stricklin

Copyright © 2015 by Deborah Rae Stricklin

Cover design by Martijn van Tilborgh

Published by Dream Releaser Publishing

Print ISBN: 978-1-943294-15-2
eBook ISBN: 978-1-943294-16-9

Come to the Mountain is also available on Amazon
Kindle, Barnes & Noble Nook and Apple iBooks.

Contents

Introduction

FOR MANY YEARS, I have been fascinated with the term "the mountain of God" in Scripture. This traditionally refers to places such as Mount Sinai, Mount Moriah, and Mount Zion, which have taken on significance as places where people sought refuge in God's presence. In my study of Scripture references to these physical locations, I discovered the beauty of peace and rest as God draws His children to Himself. The chapters that follow are glimpses into the lives of Bible heroes beckoned by God into His presence. His purpose in drawing us to Himself is always to knit our hearts with His. In pursuit of the Christian walk, our influence would be much greater if we would simply make Jesus Christ the focus of our desires. If we'll have the courage to respond when He calls, our lives will be forever changed. It is my joy to share with you how my own life has been significantly impacted by His call to me to *Come to the Mountain*. I pray yours will be as well.

Chapter One

A Place of Rest

"The Lord is my Shepherd; I have everything I need. He lets me rest in green meadows; he leads me beside peaceful streams. He renews my strength. He guides me along right paths, bringing honor to his name. Even when I walk through the darkest valley, I will not be afraid, for you are close beside me. Your rod and your staff protect and comfort me." — Psalm 23:1-4 (NLT)

I HAVE ALWAYS LOVED the twenty-third Psalm. It seems that this psalm has become a mourner's psalm, being used primarily at funerals; but, I've always seen it as a life-psalm, one that speaks wisdom about God's design for the ebb and flow of life.

This sin-filled world naturally leads us to a hamster-wheel existence. We work ourselves into a rut, allow our expenses to exceed our income, and then work harder, thinking if we labor just a little more, somehow we'll magically get ahead. But, this is not God's desire for us.

God instituted the Sabbath for a reason. He knew we would need rest; not just for the purpose of a physical respite, but for the opportunity to renew our perspective. And, keeping the Sabbath is not a suggestion. Exodus 31:12-15 (NLT) is clearly a directive.

The Lord gave these further instructions to Moses: "Tell the people of Israel to keep my Sabbath day, for the Sabbath is a sign of the covenant between me and you forever. *It helps you to remember that I am the LORD, who makes you holy.* Yes, keep the Sabbath day, for it is holy. Anyone who desecrates it must die; anyone who works on that day will be cut off from the community. Work six days only, but the seventh day must be a day of total rest. I repeat: Because the LORD considers it a holy day, anyone who works on the Sabbath must be put to death." (italics mine)

We don't put people to death these days for working on the Sabbath, but the principle behind this Mosaic law is that one day a week must be set aside as holy. The Sabbath is a day centered on God for the purpose of worship, rest, and renewing perspective. We so easily become entangled with work productivity and money-making that God made an enforced day to course-correct our thinking. Godly rest is crucial to maintaining our focus on the Kingdom of God. The day-to-day issues we encounter have a way of ordering our responses, and God's Sabbath reestablishes our center on Him and His Word.

If we maintain a life-style of busyness and fail to institute a Sabbath day in our week, we fall prey to losing sight of Kingdom importance. Neglecting rest over a long period of time leads to a downward spiral physically, mentally, and spiritually that is difficult to climb out of. If we will obey God's principles, whether they are convenient or not, God faithfully blesses us in unexpected ways. These God-given principles are just as necessary today as they were back in the time of Moses and the Exodus from Egypt, which is where we'll start our journey of learning God's rest.

As the Israelites exited Egypt, they needed a time of purposeful rest focused on re-learning the ways of the Lord. At the foot of Mount Sinai, the Israelites camped for over a year while God gave Moses the laws for His people to live by. He was deliberately transforming their thinking. They had been slaves in Egypt for four hundred years. Mom and Dad had been slaves. Grandpa and Grandma had been slaves. As a matter of fact, as far back as any of the Israelites could remember, they had an ancestry of slavery to the Egyptians. The days of walking in the blessings of God on behalf of His children were distant stories retold by each generation. Moving the people from a slave mentality into freedom as God's children was not an overnight job. The Hebrew heritage their ancestors practiced had to be reestablished. They needed to be governed by a set of boundaries that would help them learn to live in freedom without harming themselves. God had rescued them from the Egyptians, and with an eye to the future, He was preparing them for what lay ahead. God had spoken beautiful promises yet to come—a land of bountiful blessing. But, without a time of restful preparation and renewed purpose, their blessing would easily become a snare to their families.

Part of the difficulty we add to our own lives is that we don't take the opportunities of rest that God offers. You may say, "Debbie, I've been running myself ragged, and I haven't seen opportunities of rest." God has not passed you by. Our mistake is that we expect a period of rest to be offered to us on a silver platter. All of our finances will be in order, our relationships will be friction-less, and we can "play" our way through God's assigned rest in our lives. Honestly, if that's what you're looking for, you've missed God's intent. He just doesn't operate that way. If our focus is on ourselves, we've missed the point all together. God offers rest, but we must watch carefully for it and treat that time as set apart for Him.

My offer of rest came at an extremely inconvenient time. For several years, I had been teaching in a private school, giving my children a Christian education. My older two children had graduated and gone off to college. My son was finishing his sophomore year in high school when God prompted me to resign my position. My husband had received a small severance package from his long-term employer some months prior to God's request for rest in my life. He hadn't been able to find a job and was working two part-time jobs, and God had the audacity to suggest that I resign!

With God's incredible grace (and my husband's permission), I left my position, trusting that He had a plan I just couldn't see. I fully expected to walk into the next phase of my life, complete with a paycheck, within just a few months. God had other plans. It took about three months for me to realize that I wasn't in a short transition from career to career. I had been ushered into a period of rest and renewal.

So, I spent the next three years at the foot of Mount Sinai. God had much work to do in me to prepare me for what lay ahead. Once I realized that this was a time of restful change and restoration, I leaned into His process. I have to admit, though, that each month felt like it was the last, and then off I'd go into the next life-phase. Admittedly, I've always been like a race horse at the gate! Even after I had come to love and treasure this time with the Lord, there still remained a restlessness to continue moving. I was learning to live in the balance of resting in His presence, yet anticipating what was to come.

In every way, God's assigned rest in my life came at great sacrifice. Anything worth obtaining requires sacrifice, especially in the Kingdom of God. Financially, this time of coming aside was a constant battle. It seemed going back to work was the obvious answer, but it wasn't God's answer. That was tough. However, God remained faithful to sustain my family. I had a strong sense that this period of time was so critical, that it was worth whatever sacrifice had to be made. Relationally, my marriage had been through some rough waters, and God was using this period of rest to heal my heart. My children were constantly coming and going from college to home, and the goodbyes for months on end were never easy. The dreams God had deposited in my spirit had become seasoned hopes within me, though they still lay just beyond my reach. My time spent in God's presence became my most precious possession. God never wastes our experiences, and what He has used mine to accomplish for Himself has amazed me.

Six months into my assigned rest, I began writing. As an avid reader and educator, words hold an incredible beauty for me. I had no idea writing would be part of my assignment at this stage of my life. I certainly could see myself writing later, but God had decided now was the appointed time. My first manuscript, *The Journey,* didn't take long to get on paper. When God told me to sit down and write, He wasn't messing around. *He* gave me the words for that book. I know that for two reasons—the words came quickly (like a flood), and I have re-read the manuscript numerous times to encourage myself in my own dreaming process. Those were God's words that He used to strengthen me while writing for others. That's beautiful!

A few months later, God laid *Come to the Mountain* on my heart. As His people, we are in desperate need of rest and peace. And, as He has led me into His rest, a path has been created which others can follow. When God calls us aside, we don't know all that He has in mind for us. We have a tendency to want the details upfront, but that's rarely how God operates. Allow Him to call you into rest. Your rest won't look exactly like my rest. Each of us is unique in our calling and preparation, and God deals with us based on what will best benefit His Kingdom.

And, most recently, I completed *The Tempted.* The longing of our hearts, unrealized to most of us, is filled in the depth of His love. What drives us to fulfill that longing so often leads us into sin rather than into His presence. If we'll hide ourselves in Him, His love satiates our deepest unmet needs.

Back to the book at hand, I began this chapter with a passage from Psalm 23.

The Lord is my Shepherd; I have everything I need. He lets me rest in green meadows; he leads me beside peaceful streams. He renews my strength. He guides me along right paths, bringing honor to his name. Even when I walk through the darkest valley, I will not be afraid, for you are close beside me. Your rod and your staff protect and comfort me (verses 1-4, NLT).

King David, the author of this Psalm, had learned through great difficulty to rely on God's leading and guidance. He experienced the benefits of trusting God in his darkest and most confusing moments. David had spent much time tending sheep alone in the wilderness. And, that atmosphere was conducive to conversation with the Almighty. Talking with God became as natural to David as caring for the sheep. As David listened, God's voice became discernible, a beautiful outcome of spending time with Him. Learning to recognize God's voice is critical for us, as well, in following Him.

John 10 is the New Testament reflection on Psalm 23. Jesus is teaching the people in this passage, revealing more of Himself to them. Although God's Hebrew name Jehovah Ro'i first appears in Psalm 23, we learn more about this aspect of God in His Son, Jesus, in John 10. Jehovah Ro'i is translated *God my Shepherd,* or *God Sees.* This name refers to His leadership and care over our lives, as a shepherd would lead his flock. In Psalm 23, we see how He leads us into rest and nourishment. Jesus, in John 10, takes His role as Shepherd even further.

The sheep hear His voice and come to Him. He calls His own sheep by name and leads them out. After He has gathered His own flock, He walks ahead of them, and they follow Him because they recognize IIis voice (vv. 3b-4, NLT).

Jesus describes His role as Shepherd as protective and sacrificial.

I am the good shepherd. The good shepherd lays down his life for the sheep. A hired hand will run when he sees a wolf coming. He will leave the sheep because they aren't his and he isn't their shepherd. And so the wolf attacks them and scatters the flock. The hired hand runs away because he is merely hired and has no real concern for the sheep. I am the good shepherd; I know my own sheep, and they know me, just as my Father knows me and I know the Father. And I lay down my life for the sheep. — John 10:11-15 (NLT)

More than one shepherd would bring his sheep into a sheepfold (fenced area) for the night. A gatekeeper would guard the gate, only allowing the shepherds to come through. Sheep are vulnerable, but their ability to learn the voice of their shepherd is uncanny. The shepherds file into the sheepfold, calling their sheep. From among the intermingled flocks, a shepherd's sheep will respond to his voice and come out. They will follow without hesitation. Our ability to successfully follow our Shepherd depends on our willingness to learn His voice.

Periods of assigned rest help us quiet ourselves before Him, and in the stillness, He can be heard. He is always guiding us, but we aren't always listening. When we begin to hold as precious the moments in life we can simply sit in His presence, we are finally learning what it means to follow Him. Our obedience, our steadfastness, and our faithfulness are bound up in the beauty of His glorious presence. If you are struggling in your relationship with the Lord, ask Him to draw you into His rest where your heart can be knit inseparably to His.

Chapter Two

A Place of Refuge

"Send me your light and your faithful care, let them lead me; let them bring me to your holy mountain, to the place where you dwell." — Psalm 43:3 (NIV)

No MATTER HOW many years we've logged as Christ-followers, there are moments when this life overwhelms us. The loss of a job, the sickness or death of a loved one, or well-laid plans that simply blow up can leave us feeling lost and alone. Even if we're not prone to fear, fearfulness can sneak up on us when we least expect it in the middle of tough circumstances.

This is exactly what happened to Elijah. 1 Kings 17-19 gives us a brief window into Elijah's humanity. By God's command, Elijah approached King Ahab, an evil king of Israel, to inform him that it would not rain on the land again until Elijah gave the word. Three years of severe drought followed. God hid Elijah during this time because Ahab was angry and sought his life. At God's timing three years later, Elijah presented himself before Ahab to inform him it would soon rain. So that God's name would receive the credit, Elijah challenged Ahab's prophets of Baal to a showdown on Mount Carmel. Each prepared a sacrifice. The prophets of Baal would call on their god to produce the fire for their sacrifice. And, Elijah would call on his God to produce the fire for *his* sacrifice. Whichever one answered would be declared the true God. Of course, Baal lost, and God won! Elijah and the Israelite bystanders seized the prophets of Baal and killed them all. What happened next is of interest to us.

God sent the rain, and one would think Ahab and his wife, Jezebel, would be pleased. However, Jezebel was furious about the prophets being killed. She vowed to hunt Elijah to his death. After such a mighty display of faith and God's power, we might expect Elijah to stand as a tower of strength against Jezebel's threat. Instead, he was afraid, and he bolted. He ran into the wilderness and hid under a tree. An angel ministered to him twice throughout the night with food and water to sustain him for the long journey ahead. God strengthened him and beckoned him to Himself, to the mountain of God.

He got up and ate and drank, and the food gave him enough strength to travel forty days and forty nights to Mount Sinai, the mountain of God (1 Kings 19:8, NLT).

When Elijah's faith was weak, God brought him to Himself at the mountain.

From our human perspective, life can get pretty scary. Even when we're prayed up, we can sometimes get caught off guard. God doesn't forget our frailty but instead offers us a place of refuge in Himself. I love His watchful care over our lives. If we'll come to Him in humility, He will meet us at the point of our need and breathe His life into us once again. I love how God ministered to Elijah on the mountain.

"Go out and stand before me on the mountain," the Lord told him. And as Elijah stood there, the Lord passed by, and a mighty windstorm hit the mountain. It was such a terrible blast that the rocks were torn loose, but the Lord was not in the wind. After the wind there was an earthquake, but the Lord was not in the earthquake. And after the earthquake there was a fire, but the Lord was not in the fire. And after the fire there was the sound of a gentle whisper. When Elijah heard it, he wrapped his face in his cloak and went out and stood at the entrance of the cave. —1 Kings 19:11-13 (NLT)

God loudly established His strength, but He quietly spoke to Elijah's heart. Comfort and peace washed over Elijah at the beautiful sound of his Lord's voice.

We may not have a mountain to run to, but the humility of a quieted heart is what God seeks. We allow our lives to consistently remain too loud and too busy. We often miss our opportunity to hear His quieting voice.

When we encounter moments of devastation or confusion, will we take the time to withdraw and sit in His presence? I have watched people look to everyone else except God for the answers they so desperately seek.

Our social network systems and readily available communication makes connecting with people so much more convenient than connecting with God. No one else is able to offer us a place of refuge as God can. He alone is our shield and strength.

When we allow other voices to speak into our situation, we dilute the impact of God's words to us. God may give us people we can go to for words of wisdom, but He desires us to come to Him first. If we'll hear His instructions at the outset, the words of others become either confirmation or simply not applicable. I would rather have one word from the throne of God than a thousand words from the lips of people.

He not only comforts us in those quiet moments, but also directs us forward. We receive instructions so we may proceed in faith. God's words of quiet care to Elijah included his next steps.

Then the Lord told (Elijah), "Go back the way you came, and travel to the wilderness of Damascus. When you arrive there, anoint Hazael to be king of Aram. Then anoint Jehu son of Nimshi to be king of Israel, and anoint Elisha son of Shaphat from Abel-meholah to replace you as my prophet." —1 Kings 19:15-16 (NLT)

Elijah had served God faithfully, and his time as God's prophet to the people of Israel was drawing to a close. God gave Elijah the name of his successor, as He had done for Moses. God's instructions to us are critical in knowing and carrying out His will, and we must be willing to immerse ourselves in His presence, gaining needed direction and strength.

So many people who say they are God-followers don't truly see God as their refuge and source. They believe Him to be an overbearing parent or a wish-granting genie, but few see Him as their shelter. Ever since I was little, I've always viewed God as my loving Father. I knew that I brought pleasure to Him; not because of anything I had done, but simply because He created me and breathed life into me. He smiles over my life simply because I belong to Him. As His child, I never sensed disapproval from Him. If I sinned, I tried to fix it because I didn't like feeling separated from Him. The funny thing is, I thought all Christians felt the same way about Him. As I've gotten older and have listened to more people's stories, I've come to realize that actually very few people see God as the loving Father He is. Honestly, that has surprised me.

It's often our perception of Him that He deals with when we come to Him as our refuge. We come broken and hurting. We want Him to resolve our problems, but instead, He reveals more of Himself to us. How does that help? It forces us to put our problems into perspective with eternity.

I have always been a go-getter. If God put a future picture in my heart, I would pursue it. Taking a back seat to achievement has never been my problem! However, letting God lead me certainly has. In these three years of coming aside with the Lord, He has slowed me down and re-prioritized my perspective. My foremost goal has become to know Him. My highest achievement is in practicing His presence. That doesn't mean I don't have goals and ambition.

It simply means that I wait for Him to usher in His plans rather than kicking doors open outside of His timing.

When God looks at our lives, He sees the long view. He was planning for our birth before our conception, and He was planning for our eternity before our salvation. Our eighty-something years on planet Earth are just a small precursor to an eternal existence with the very One who creatively formed us and gave us life. God waits for us to need Him. He longs for us to run to Him. Our independence and self-reliance are not at all signs of maturity. The peace and quiet strength that come from reliance on Him are true signs of maturity. Our hearts should desire to echo King David's words,

> I love you, Lord; you are my strength. The Lord is my rock, my fortress, and my savior; my God is my rock, in whom I find protection. He is my shield, the strength of my salvation, and my stronghold. — Psalm 18:1-2 (NLT)

We all need a rescuer, a source of strength far greater than ourselves. If we'll come to Him as our refuge, He'll renew our perspective and give us direction and vigor to begin moving again. We may emerge with problems still intact, but our approach to those problems will be effectively different.

Chapter Three

A Place of Redirection

"Now go, for I am sending you to Pharaoh. You will lead my people, the Israelites, out of Egypt." — Exodus 3:10 (NLT)

MOSES, ONE OF the greatest leaders in history, stumbled into a moment of wilderness redirection in the foothills of Mount Sinai. He didn't become known for his leadership skills until he was well into his eighties. The first forty years of his life had been spent as a son of royalty in Pharaoh's palace. Of Hebrew birth, Moses' newfound identification with his people brought a breach in his relationship with Pharaoh. Running for his life, Moses spent the next forty years in the wilderness with a group of God-fearing Midianite people where he married and settled into a life of shepherding.

Moses wasn't looking for a revelatory experience with God at the age of eighty. According to Scripture, it appears that the burning bush experience took Moses rather by surprise.

> One day Moses was tending the flock of his father-in-law, Jethro, the priest of Midian, and he went deep into the wilderness near Sinai, the mountain of God. Suddenly, the angel of the Lord appeared to him as a blazing fire in a bush. Moses was amazed because the bush was engulfed in flames, but it didn't burn up... When the Lord saw that he had caught Moses' attention, God called to him from the bush, "Moses! Moses!" —Exodus 3:1-2, 4 (NLT)

This was the first of many times in Moses' future that God would manifest Himself in fire. I love how God starts small (with a bush), and then progresses to full-out (the top of a mountain is ablaze later!).

After forty years of quiet shepherding in the wilderness, God was ready to take Moses on a journey of unmatched proportion. God had taken all of Moses' experiences and packaged them together as preparation for leading two million people out of Pharaoh's grip into wilderness living (for another forty years) on their way to the Promised Land.

God does that, you know! He uses the experiences from our lives that have been so hurtful and confusing to mold us to His purpose. The pain we endure surely seems to us to be wasted effort. Whether we or others caused our pain, we have a difficult time seeing its purpose.

There is a story I love that well illustrates the benefit of our bitter experiences. An elderly woman tells of her childhood, "When I was a little girl in Germany, one day I asked my mother what it means that 'all things work together for good.' My mother was baking a cake and, without directly answering my question, she handed me a spoonful of baking soda. It tasted awful. Finally, I asked her what she was doing and she responded that she was answering my question. 'Amelia,' my mother said, 'I don't want you to ever forget that all things taken by themselves are not always pleasant. But when they are mixed together and fired in the oven, you love the results.'" (*A Psalm in Your Heart,* p.127)

The Scripture to which the woman's mother is referring is Romans 8:28 (NLT),

And we know that God causes everything to work together for the good of those who love God and are called according to his purpose for them.

I'll be the first to admit that difficult circumstances can be bitter indeed, but it's critical that we focus our attention on Jesus during those times rather than on the circumstances themselves. If we can keep moving through the difficulty, He'll weave together the bad and the good until what emerges surprises even us. This beautiful poem reminds us that God uses what we view as hurtful experiences to construct a life of greater purpose.

My life is but a weaving between my Lord and me;
I cannot choose the colors,
He worketh steadily.
Oft times He weaveth sorrow,
And I in foolish pride,
Forget He sees the upper,
And I the underside.

Not 'til the loom is silent
And the shuttles cease to fly,
Shall God unroll the canvas
And explain the reason why.
The dark threads are as needful
In the Weaver's skillful hand,
As the threads of gold and silver
In the pattern He has planned.
He knows, He loves, He cares,
Nothing this truth can dim,
He gives the very best to those
Who leave the choice with Him.

—Author Unknown

The last two lines are the most beautiful in my opinion. "He gives the very best to those who leave the choice with Him." God certainly doesn't inflict pain and suffering in our lives, but He does, at times, allow it. And, He reserves His greatest favor and blessings for those who don't try to escape the pain, but instead embrace trusting Him to decide when difficulty would best benefit what He's doing in and through our lives.

James goes even further to say, "...whenever trouble comes your way, let it be an opportunity for joy. For when your faith is tested, your endurance has a chance to grow. So let it grow, for when your endurance is fully developed, you will be strong in character and ready for anything" (James 1:2-4, NLT).

As affliction has crowded its way into my life, I haven't always seen it as a benefit. But, these verses in James clearly tell us that God allows trouble in our lives for the purpose of maturing us. Knowing that should give us the courage to say, "Let the trials come." There is a trust factor that is tested in the midst of trials. Do we trust that the God who allowed the trial will indeed carry us through it? If we'll take hold of the solid fact that He is completely faithful and trustworthy, we can confidently keep walking through the fiery trial, assured we will emerge stronger on the other side of deliverance.

When God calls us to His purposes, and we respond, Satan takes the threat personally. He often will apply the full-court press to our lives hoping to dissuade us from following God's call. In my life, as I wholeheartedly responded to the Lord's call to preach His gospel, the enemy of God released flaming arrow after flaming arrow, trying to distract and destroy God's plan. My marriage was one area hit hard by the onslaught. Five years of fighting to save what appeared dead was weighing heavily on me. God gave me a beautiful Scripture in the midst of the struggle.

> Now I will relieve your shoulder of its burden; I will free your hands from their heavy tasks. You cried to me in trouble, and I saved you: I answered out of the thundercloud. I tested your faith at Meribah...
> — Psalm 81:6-7 (NLT)

Meribah represents a place of potential bitterness. The Israelites, upon leaving Egypt, complained against the Lord at Meribah because there was no water. God was their Provider, but instead of asking Him for what they needed, they complained and blamed God for their thirst.

Our trials are opportunities the Lord uses to test our reliance on Him and our resolve to trust Him. In my marriage, I knew my assignment over those years was to simply not give up. Although I had very little control over the situation, I could pray and remain faithful. God was watching for my response to the difficulty. I found a place to hide myself in Him until He resolved the situation. Psalm 81:6-7 was given to me during that five year period, but deliverance from the difficulty didn't come immediately. My job was to believe that God would somehow come through in His own timing. Through a series of events, my husband and I ended up in a three-day marriage counseling session where God put His miraculous hand of healing on our marriage. What appeared dead had been resurrected. He is so faithful! As I look back on the last few years, the onslaught of the enemy has been relentless, but the power of the Living God has been stronger, and I marvel at how He has used Satan's efforts to mature me. I feel like a different person, completely reliant on and confident in the greatness of my Savior. This is always His purpose in allowing pain in our lives—to mature us and make us more like Himself. Knowing this gives us the ability to praise Him in the midst of our devastating circumstances.

There is a passage in Deuteronomy that I have come to love.

Remember how the Lord your God led you through the wilderness for forty years, *humbling you and testing you to prove your character,* and to find out whether or not you would really obey his commands. Yes, *he humbled you by letting you go hungry and then feeding you with manna,* a food previously unknown to you and your ancestors. He did it to teach you that people need more than bread for their life; *real life comes by feeding on every word of the Lord.* — Deut. 8:2-3 (NLT, italics mine)

Are you willing to let God humble you? Will you cooperate with Him when He "lets you go hungry" and then gives you what you need rather than what you want?

As I mentioned earlier, during the past five years, God removed from my life all that I thought I needed and replaced it with what He has chosen for me. The first three of those five years were years of confusion because I didn't understand what was happening. I felt like the victim of a Job experience. My marriage careened into what seemed the deepest chasm, my children began their pilgrimages away from me and into adult life, our finances plunged into devastation, my only extended family moved across the country, people who I had come to trust abandoned me, and my God-given dream took a left-turn toward a life-threatening cliff. It seemed things were coming apart faster than I could put them back together.

The rapidity of the onslaught of difficulty felt like unrelenting, overpowering ocean waves. Once I realized that my ability to control my circumstances was gone, I began to relax into the arms of the only One who could save me from drowning in the hardship and heartache. I chose to stop flailing in my attempt to keep my head above the waves and let *Him* decide when I'd had enough. As Christians, we love to say that He won't put more on us than we can bear. But, *our* idea of what we can bear and *His* idea of what we can bear are completely different. I decided that I wanted to find out what the blessing would be if I chose to let Him take me to *His* limit rather than my own. We are so much stronger in Christ than we realize. We cut our blessings short when we think the pain is too great and bail out during difficulty. My goal became to simply keep telling Him, "If *You* say that I can keep going, then I can keep going. Fill me with your joy so I'll be strong enough to endure." It's a blind walk into the unknown, but if you trust the One who's doing the leading, you're in good hands!

So, Moses began his journey into the unknown as the leader of an enslaved people whom he hadn't seen in forty years. God instructed Moses,

> You can be sure I have seen the misery of my people in Egypt. I have heard their cries for deliverance from their harsh slave drivers. Yes, I am aware of their suffering. So I have come to rescue them from the Egyptians and lead them out of Egypt into their own good and spacious land. It is a land flowing with milk and honey—the land where the Canaanites, Hittites, Amorites, Perizzites, Hivites, and Jebusites live. The cries of the people of Israel have reached me, and I have seen how the Egyptians have oppressed them with heavy tasks. Now go, for I am sending you to Pharaoh. You will lead my people, the Israelites, out of Egypt. — Exodus 3:7-10 (NLT)

Moses' response reflected his self-doubt.

> ... Moses asked God, "How can you expect me to lead the Israelites out of Egypt?" (Exodus 3:11, NLT)

But, God never expects us to do in our own strength what He's purposed for us.

> Then God told him, "I will be with you. And this will

serve as proof that I have sent you: When you have brought the Israelites out of Egypt, you will return here to worship God *at this very mountain.*" — Exodus 3:12 (NLT, italics mine)

Don't miss this because this is beautiful— God called Moses aside, redirected his next steps, and then confirmed His words by telling Moses that he'll return to this very place *with the promise in hand* (namely, more than two million people)!

What's God trying to redirect in your life? Are you allowing Him to call you aside to a place of redirection? Whatever you focus on is the direction in which you'll move. As a gymnast growing up, the balance beam was my least favorite event. I was tall for a gymnast, and it was a long way down from the high beam! Attempting aerials, back handsprings, and tumbling passes on that four inch wide beam seemed tortuous. The key to maintaining balance atop that perch was to focus on the end point. With every move, refocusing my eyes at the end of the beam kept me from losing balance. In many cases, first place ended up going to the gymnast who simply didn't fall off during her routine. Maintaining spiritual focus is just as crucial. And, spending time with Him is the only way of obtaining proper focus. Let God set your focus. It may take sacrifice and endurance to shift your focus and obtain His promises, but anything accomplished with Kingdom purpose is worth the pain and time invested.

We must be willing to allow God access to redirect us, and there is simply no way to hear God's drawing voice in the middle of a hurried life. You are the only one who can choose to quiet yourself before Him. It *is* a choice, and God won't demand His way in your life. Choosing to cooperate with His methods requires being with Him enough that you learn to trust Him. There is no substitution for time in His presence. His call to you to come aside, to come to the mountain, is a lifeline to weather the storms He knows are coming your way. Will you have the courage to follow His lead? Will you give in to the unrelenting call of unfinished tasks or will you respond to the unmistakable call of your Heavenly Father's voice? The choice is yours. Your future and the future of those you're assigned to influence hang in the balance. Choose Him!

Chapter Four

A Place of Reclamation

*" 'And the Sovereign Lord says: I will take a tender shoot from the top of a tall cedar, and I will plant it on the top of Israel's highest mountain. It will become a noble cedar, sending forth its branches and producing seed. Birds of every sort will nest in it, finding shelter beneath its branches. And all the trees will know that it is I, the Lord, who cuts down the tall tree and helps the short tree to grow tall. It is I who makes the green tree wither and gives new life to the dead tree. I, the Lord, have spoken! I will do what I have said.'" —
Ezekiel 17:22-24 (NLT)*

G OD IS IN THE business of reclaiming what is His. The hard truth is, we, as humans, go astray. Although He is faithful, we are not. No matter how devoted our hearts are to our Lord, sin is always crouching at the door, ready to draw us away in thought or in deed. But, God never gives up. According to Noah

Webster's 1828 *American Dictionary of the English Language,* the definition of reclaim is 1) to demand that something be returned 2) to call back from error, wandering, or transgression 3) to recall. God pursues to reclaim what is His and breathes new life even into what appears dead.

Throughout the Old Testament, Israel made a habit of straying. She would, like her neighbors, begin to worship other gods. God would punish her because of her disobedience, and the people would cry out to the Lord for help. As humans, two or three cycles of this would provoke us to drop kick Israel right out the back door. Not so with God. His amazing, unfailing love and the honor of His name just keep coming back for her *and* for us. Although originally spoken over Israel, the following passage in Ezekiel reminds us of the power of God's reclamation:

> Then I will sprinkle clean water on you, and you will be clean. Your filth will be washed away, and you will no longer worship idols. And I will give you a new heart with new and right desires, and I will put a new spirit in you. I will take out your stony heart of sin and give you a new, obedient heart. And I will put my Spirit in you so you will obey my laws and do whatever I command. — Ezekiel 36:25-27 (NLT)

Satan's primary objective is to steal, kill, and destroy. He accomplishes this through deception, separating and isolating that which was originally God's creation. Conversely, God's objective is to bring us back to Himself, where we will enjoy the blessings of His presence and abundance. And, He accomplishes this through wooing, loving chastisement, and discipline. God desires to bless us; Satan desires to destroy us. What Satan has stolen, God reclaims.

Land reclamation is an interesting parallel. When the trees in a forest or field are cut down, the soil is left exposed. The soil is severely affected by drought conditions, high winds, and heavy rains. The trees naturally growing in the forests and fields protected the vulnerable soil (the source of nourishment for plant life) from exposure and erosion. In order to reverse the damage brought on by drought, wind, and rain, trees are strategically planted to provide stability and protection for the soil.

In our lives, whether through sin or circumstance, Satan comes in and clear-cuts our resources and stability, hoping to leave us vulnerable and exposed. But, as we hide ourselves in the Lord, He replants what was stripped away, bringing us comfort, life, and peace. Satan strips; God reclaims.

You may feel like a victim of Satan's stripping. Perhaps you've lost a job that has been your source for a long time. Or, your marriage unexpectedly has spiraled into chaos. Your kids may be making unwise and detrimental decisions. A dream that was given to you by God Himself may, from all outward indications, appear completely decimated. It's in those unsettling moments that God is offering us an opportunity to see His reclamation efforts at work!

Eighteen years have passed since God deposited His future plans for my life in my heart. Life was progressing through the raising of children, career advancement, ministerial credentialing, and growth in ministry. Then, within a short time, my job was gone, my children were launched, my marriage crashed, and I was side-lined from ministry. I had opportunity to lay blame on those who had harmed me, but God redirected my attention toward Himself. When God brings us to a place of dryness, it's important to recognize that He is using the circumstances to re-center us and prepare us for what lies ahead. Blaming others will only stall the process God is working in you. Looking to Him will give God full access to reclamation and blessing in your life. What has been declared dead will live again!

The Biblical accounts of David and Joseph immediately come to mind when discussing reclamation of God-induced dreams. As a young boy, David was anointed by Samuel to become the next king of Israel. King Saul was currently on the throne, also anointed by Samuel, to rule over God's people. King Saul came to the throne *not* preceded by testing and proving. Over time, trying situations revealed his untested character. Rather than follow the will of the Lord and work for the good of the people, he sought to protect himself and his position.

Conversely, David was given the throne preceded by almost two decades of severe character testing, mostly at the hands of Saul, whom David had served faithfully. Saul's throne was removed from him, and he died in judgment. One would think David would rejoice over Saul's demise, but instead, David wept and mourned over the wasted life of God's anointed servant. This was a man David had loved and served as his own father. Yet Saul had severely mistreated him and even sought David's life for years. David was displaced from his home, running from Saul and hiding in caves. This king-to-be hid in obscurity while Saul intentionally sought David's harm. Bitterness was at David's fingertips, available for the taking and ingesting. In wisdom, David knew bitterness would destroy God's plans for his life, and instead, chose to return love for hate.

What God had set in motion almost two decades earlier through the laying on of Samuel's hands, God would complete in His perfect timing. David understood that this was God's purpose, and his only responsibility in bringing it to pass was remaining faithful. No one would be able to keep God's plans from eventual manifestation except David himself. The character wrought in David during so many years of testing prepared him to wear the crown of Israel. He had learned to seek God's presence, finding a source of peace and strength through every storm that would serve him well during his lifetime of leadership. He became known as a man after God's own heart, not perfect, but humble. (David's story is found in 1 Samuel 16—1 Kings 2).

Joseph's circumstances led him through the same character-building wilderness. As a young teenager, Joseph dreamt that his father, mother, and brothers would bow down to him in future days. That didn't sit too well with his family. At the hands of his jealous brothers, he was sold into slavery in Egypt. By God's design, he was purchased by Potiphar, one of Pharaoh's officers.

Putting aside bitterness, Joseph chose to serve well and enjoyed promotion in Potiphar's household. That didn't last long, as Potiphar's wife wanted Joseph to join her in bed. Being a man of integrity, Joseph refused. Scorned,

Potiphar's wife accused Joseph of attempted rape. His life spiraled further from slavery to incarceration. He couldn't have been further from the fulfillment of his dream unless he was dead. Yet again, he chose forgiveness rather than bitterness. The jailer and other inmates prospered during Joseph's prison stint, and one day, Joseph was released from prison after interpreting one of Pharaoh's dreams. Again, by God's design, that very day Joseph was catapulted out of prison and into position as Pharaoh's right-hand man. Had bitterness invaded Joseph's spirit, he would not have been ready for such immediate advancement. God abundantly rewarded Joseph's humble submission to His methods of character-building. (Joseph's story is found in Genesis 37-50).

In my own life, God has begun the reclamation process. My time spent in His presence has richly nourished my spirit, enabling growth during this wilderness experience, which is the point of these dry times. Just like Joseph, we must come to the point that we say to those who have persecuted us,

> ...Don't be angry with yourselves that you did this to me, for God did it. He sent me here ahead of you to preserve your lives... Yes, it was God who sent me here, not you! — Genesis 45:5-8 (NLT)

And, if you are experiencing unjust treatment, be encouraged by 1 Peter 2:19-20 (NLT):

> For God is pleased with you when, for the sake of your conscience, you patiently endure unfair treatment. Of course, you get no credit for being patient if you are beaten for doing wrong. But if you suffer for doing right and are patient beneath the blows,

God is pleased with you.

As human beings, we all occasionally act in ways that are less than noble. Finding the courage to forgive and move forward gives us the ability to obtain those dreams that appear to be dead. God beautifully reclaims what Satan thought he had stolen from us, and ushers in His purposes. Withholding forgiveness or neglecting to let go of the past slows our progress and possibly stalls us out completely. There is no one who can stop God's delivery in progress through your life except you. That's both freeing and humbling. It's so beneficial to know that the people around you aren't controlling your destiny. And, yet, you have the responsibility to conduct yourself in obedience and integrity so God can work freely through you.

Though times of testing produce intense pressure, the refinement process yields beautiful results. Job 23:8-10 (NLT) reminds us that the process is worth the pain. Job speaks of God:

> I go east, but he is not there. I go west, but I cannot find him. I do not see him in the north, for he is hidden. I turn to the south, but I cannot find him. *He knows where I am going,* and when he has tested me like gold in a fire, he will pronounce me innocent. (italics mine)

In the midst of accusation, pressure, pain, and betrayal, your greatest asset is peace with your Savior. *He knows where you are going.* And, He is the only One who can part the Red Sea for you and light the way. The scripture in Job says, "And when he has tested me like gold in a fire, he will pronounce me innocent" (v. 10, NLT).

You will emerge from the refining process beautiful, pure, and innocent by the mouth of God. That is reason for celebration!

Chapter Five

A Place of Restoration

"These are the instructions for the whole burnt offering, the grain offering, the sin offering, the guilt offering, the ordination offering, and the peace offering. The Lord gave these instructions to Moses on Mount Sinai when he commanded the Israelites to bring their offerings to the Lord in the wilderness of Sinai." — Leviticus 7:37-38 (NLT)

STILL CAMPED AT the foot of Mt. Sinai, Moses delivered the Lord's sacrificial instructions to the Israelite people. The tabernacle had been constructed, and sacrifices were being instituted, both in procedure and purpose. The book of Leviticus serves as a window into the daily lives of these people God claimed as His very own children. The overwhelming theme of Leviticus is sacrifice.

God was teaching the people from the onset of their journey that He must remain at the center of their lives and that He is holy. Sin must be dealt with, and the only acceptable payment is the spilling of blood. Animal sacrifices were daily occurrences among God's children. The sacrificial animal represented the giving of one life for the saving of another. The animal took the sinner's place and paid the penalty for the sin committed.

The whole point of sacrifice was to provide a way to seek forgiveness from sin-induced separation and restore relationship with God. Sacrifice was God's temporary solution, knowing all the while that the permanent solution was on the way—the ultimate sacrifice of His Son, Jesus Christ. Because of His death, our sins have been completely forgiven, and our fellowship with God has been restored!

Jesus beckons us to follow His example and live with completely surrendered hearts to Him. If blood sacrifices are no longer necessary because of Jesus, how, then, do we live sacrificial lives? Romans 8:6 (NLT) tells us,

> If your sinful nature controls your mind, there is death. But if the Holy Spirit controls your mind, there is life and peace.

Turning control of our minds over to the Holy Spirit requires more than our consent. It requires the sacrifice of our time and devotion.

We, as God's creation, are divided into three parts: spirit, soul, and body. Your spirit is your direct line to the Holy Spirit. Your soul is your mind, will, and emotions through which you process what the world throws your direction. Your body is your physical person, the flesh and bone "house" in which your spirit and soul reside. Picture your three parts as concentric circles: the innermost circle is your spirit, the middle circle is your soul (mind, will, and emotions), and the outer circle is your body (flesh). Everything coming from the world must be processed through your flesh, filtered by your soul, and finally deposited in your spirit. Everything coming from the Holy Spirit bypasses the body and soul and is deposited directly into your spirit.

Your soul (mind, will, and emotions), then, becomes the contested domain. You have the world's input which came by way of your flesh, and you have the Holy Spirit's influence which came by way of your spirit. Whichever you allow to dominate is what will control your sense of life and peace. Let's re-read Romans 8:6 (NLT): "If your sinful nature controls your mind, there is death. But if the Holy Spirit controls your mind, there is life and peace." So, how do we position ourselves to have a Holy Spirit-controlled mind?

This is where sacrifice comes in—sacrifice of our time, schedules, self-importance, and world-influenced thinking to make room for Him. We live in a world that constantly competes for our attention, some things self-induced, and some outside of our control. And, God waits. He waits to be chosen. He waits to be pursued. Taking care of the business at hand seems so much easier than spending time with Him. Solving our own situations seems so much more direct and productive than taking the time to listen for *His* solutions. But, rarely are our solutions His solutions. Rarely are our business outcomes His business outcomes. We are too easily satisfied with the wrong things. We've settled for the world's level of living rather than God's level of blessing.

God gives us a choice. Will we keep pace with the world, or will we follow His bidding to come away with Him? In 2009, God began to draw me toward a more intensive prayer life. I was teaching school full-time, volunteering much time at church, working on my ministerial studies, training for my first half-marathon, and still had all three of my children at home. Spending more time in prayer would appear to be counter-productive to a busy life, but the exact opposite is true. As God pressed me to carve more time out of my day for Him, I settled on the only available uninterrupted time in my day—during the early morning hours when most people are still sleeping. I began my 4:00am prayer time with determination. It had to become a habit, so excuses were not an option. This early morning time gave me about an hour and a half to be in His presence before starting my day. My hunger for hearing His voice and reading His Word continued to increase as time went on. By the end of 2012, He had become so much the object of my affection that everything else in my life felt like it was competing for my time with Him. The opportunity that I have taken over the last three years to completely devote myself to spending time in His presence has changed my life. Resigning my job at His bidding appeared radical to those who know me. They watched with trepidation. Had I lost all sense of reality? In the midst of their concern, I clung to what I knew had been the whisper of my Lord. Following Him was *my* only consideration.

As those concerned observed my life over the next three years, they joyfully acknowledged the rise in confidence, influence, and peace. The general approval is appreciated, but few people are truly aware of the discipline and sacrifice involved. Each morning, you'll find me on my knees pouring my heart out before my Creator, my Friend, my loving Savior. I listen with desire to know His thoughts, His intentions, and His directions.

Over the years, my prayer time has grown as the Lord has impressed on me what should be added as I pray. I have benefited from listening to others pray during my own maturing process, so I'll take a few moments to let you "listen in" on some of the subjects of my prayers. When my children were little, I began praying Psalm 91 as a covering over them. As they got a little older, I started praying Psalm 112:1-3 (NLT) over their lives.

Praise the Lord! Happy are those who fear the Lord. Yes, happy are those who delight in doing what he commands. Their children will be successful everywhere; an entire generation of godly people will be blessed. They themselves will be wealthy, and their good deeds will never be forgotten.

I would remind them that being average wasn't an option because the Word of God said my children would be successful everywhere, and they would be an incredible blessing to the people around them. I didn't mind the wealthy part, either! As I pray, I specifically ask for favor, and I name the people I need favor with, from current relationships to future opportunities. I ask God to search my heart, every part of it. I invite Him to shine the light of His presence on any dark corner of my heart. Luke 11:36 tells us, "If you are filled with light, with no dark corners, then your whole life will be radiant, as though a floodlight is shining on you." I, then, begin to thank Him that my life is radiant with His light. I ask Him to give me the mouth of a minister so that I might encourage others and speak His truth in love. I ask Him to help me walk in His authority and His anointing so that I bring His presence into every situation wherever I go. I want to be His hands and feet, walking through groups of people as He walked, touching lives, and ministering to hearts. I spend time praying for those in authority over me and for Jerusalem's peace and protection. I ask that God's influence through me would reach further than I could ever imagine. Those are the basics of everyday prayer, with current concerns mixed in. There is absolutely no substitute for praying in the Spirit. I ask God to use me to speak that which needs to be birthed, undergirded, or released. Occasionally, I will be impressed to pray strength and freedom for our persecuted brothers and sisters around the world. Prayer is not only a privilege, but also a discipline. When my body would rather be sleeping, my spirit urges me to rise and pray. If you want to make a difference in the Kingdom of God and push back the kingdom of darkness, you *must* pray. *I must* pray.

Making my way to the kitchen table, I sit in the quietness of the early morning hours reading His Word and watching the sun rise. My heart fills up with His thoughts over me. Tears often come easily as I'm overwhelmed by His presence and His goodness. Two hours often easily pass before I move on to an appointment or other responsibilities. At least two days a week I linger in meditation and then begin writing. Out of the overflow of my heart, words come easily. I have learned that life has a way of depleting what's inside us, and if I don't fill up, I have nothing of value to give. When we try to operate from a deficit, an emptiness, we shift from being a giver to being a taker. We become self-absorbed, and everything is suddenly about us. The center of our thoughts and actions moves from Kingdom business to *me*-business. No time spent with God is wasted time. So, get up earlier, rearrange your schedule, or do whatever you have to do to make time to be with Him. He is the joy of my life, my reason to live, and the center of my world. His presence restores what the circumstances of life take away.

I have realized that the best gift I could ever bring to the people around me is a life filled-up with God. A God-follower whose heart is overflowing with joy, faith, peace, and grace is like a beautiful ray of hope in darkness. People are drawn to those who walk confidently in God's grace. When will we care enough about the world around us that we'll fill ourselves up with the only Hope who changes lives? We must choose to stop living depleted lives. Not only is it unhealthy for us, it does no good for anyone around us. In effect, we're living for ourselves when we choose to live depleted. Let's decide to do whatever it takes to be filled-up with Him on a daily basis!

Chapter Six

A Place of Reverence

"I look up to the mountains—does my help come from there? My help comes from the Lord, who made the heavens and the earth." — Psalm 121:1-2 (NLT)

THE JEWISH PEOPLE had a tradition, founded in the Law of Moses. Yearly, they would make their way to the temple in Jerusalem to worship and bring sacrifices. Jerusalem is located at an approximate elevation of 2,500 feet, and the surrounding area sits low, creating quite a climb for these pilgrims. As families would make the pilgrimage together, they would sing a series of short psalms called Songs of Ascent. These are Psalms 120-134. Read together, they are a beautiful reminder that through the long climb of life, God becomes our hope and our reward.

Although we all journey through joys and difficulties, we each have the opportunity to choose the object of our focus. Will we set our focus on the steep and dangerous climb? Will we focus on our weariness and fear? Or, will we choose to set our eyes on the Lord, the only One who straightens the path before us and keeps our feet from stumbling? Psalm 121 (NLT) instructs us.

> I look up to the mountains –
> Does my help come from there?
> My help comes from the Lord,
> Who made the heavens and the earth!
> He will not let you stumble and fall;
> The one who watches over you will not sleep.
> Indeed, he who watches over Israel
> never tires and never sleeps.
> The Lord himself watches over you!
> The Lord stands beside you as your protective shade.
> The sun will not hurt you by day,
> Nor the moon at night.
> The Lord keeps you from all evil
> And preserves your life.
> The Lord keeps watch over you as you come and go,
> Both now and forever.

It's so easy to get drawn into the fear and darkness of our difficult circumstances. It's equally easy to get drawn into the frivolity of the ease of life. But, neither produces the eternal focus our lives so often lack. Only when we look to Him will we correctly position ourselves in an attitude of reverence that transcends the pain and pleasures of this life.

We must constantly remind ourselves that this life is not the end goal. Just as the pilgrimage to Jerusalem focused God's children on Him and His purposes, so *our* promise of Heaven focuses our lives on our Savior and His purposes. But, how do we consistently keep the hope of Heaven squarely within our line of sight?

I wish it were like a workout video; just do the exercises on this video for six weeks, and you'll have abs like steel! Just read the Word of God for thirty minutes each day for six weeks, and you'll have an eternal perspective! No such luck. Reading the Word of God every day, however, *is* the right start. As we immerse ourselves in His presence, our thinking begins to change. Thoughts of eternity that may have seemed far away and not applicable to our lives become our primary focus. The concerns of our daily world begin to take a back seat to our heavenly home. Our purposeful pursuit of God must be continued because we live in a world hostile to eternal Kingdom thinking. Remember that life and peace come from a mind controlled by the Spirit. Transferring control to Him certainly takes focused attention!

Many people say that they reverence God, but few prove it with their lives, even among Christians. Our tendency is to use portions of Scripture for our purposes and discard what doesn't lend nicely to our lives. But, how about we read the entire counsel of the Word intending to get to know this God who amazingly takes interest in us? How about serving Him because He's worth serving? How about learning what pleases Him because He's worthy of our life-long pursuit to bring Him pleasure? Our obedience bears out our reverence.

Step-by-step obedience is often overlooked as a means to peace. God knows that our tendency is to live in complacency, seeking comfort. If angst is created in our lives, we are compelled to go to any lengths to regain emotional balance. God uses this natural human tendency in our favor if we'll cooperate with Him. He allows us to begin feeling uncomfortable and restless in areas that need change. We don't like those feelings. Awareness that this may be a transition point helps us focus our attention on what God might be doing rather than attempting to solve our own discomfort. Often His instructions to us, then, require step-by-step obedience, sometimes blindly. Trusting Him to bring His intended outcome stretches our faith.

After I had been teaching school for several years, I began to experience a growing discomfort. My heart, thoughts, and attention were increasingly gravitating toward serving through the ministries of my church. My desire to teach these beautiful children was waning. I had always said that a teacher who no longer loved being in the classroom no longer belonged there. Many teachers remain for the paycheck long after their hearts have left their classrooms. I didn't want to do that to the children. If I couldn't be fully emotionally involved in their development, then my time with them needed to come to an end.

Although I desired to serve my church with complete availability, servanthood doesn't always come with a paycheck. I was faced with a monumental decision—trust God as I was hearing from Him to resign or stay in the classroom for the paycheck. Our combined income wasn't anything to shout about as it was, much less if it were reduced by a third! I chose to blindly obey God's leading. It's been almost three years since I gave up my paycheck. Although it's been a wild ride of trust, I would do it again in a heartbeat! The beautiful opportunities the Lord has presented to me have well been worth the financial sacrifice!

My son approached me before his senior year in high school began and asked me (since I wasn't currently working in a paying job) if I would help him homeschool his senior year. Since he had attended the same Christian school since third grade, I questioned him quite pointedly about the motivation for his request and the repercussions of such a decision. After hearing him out and praying for wisdom, I granted his request. I am profoundly grateful for the year my son and I spent together. I had the privilege of pouring guidance, wisdom, and teaching into his life at a new level during this time. He took advantage of his extra time, devoting himself to serving in our church and developing his God-given talents. There is no paycheck big enough to replace what this year brought.

How would I have experienced not only the opportunities of the past three years, but also the new trajectory of my future, if I had not taken a risk and responded to God when He asked me to resign? Our desire for keeping the status quo severely limits us in the Kingdom of God. I might even go so far as to say that God would rather we step out in over-exuberant faith than to sheepishly protect the familiar.

There is a story about King Saul's son, Jonathan (after whom my son is named), in 1 Samuel that I love. He makes a bold move of faith, and God jumps in for the adventure! The Philistines were Israel's nemesis. They were stronger, faster, better equipped, and they far outnumbered their Israelite enemies. However, Jonathan recognized that God was the God of the Israelites and believed He would help His children win. The two armies were at a temporary stand-off, and the Philistines were as numerous as the grains of sand on the seashore! There were only about six hundred Israelite warriors still on the battlefield. Most had gone home in fear. Jonathan observed the odds, got tired of waiting for the battle to commence, and decided to stir up a little action on his own.

"Let's go across to see those pagans," Jonathan said to his armor bearer. "Perhaps the Lord will help us, for nothing can hinder the Lord. He can win a battle whether he has many warriors or only a few!" When the Philistines saw them coming, they shouted, "Look! The Hebrews are crawling out of their holes!" Then they shouted to Jonathan, "Come up here, and we'll teach you a lesson!" "Come on, climb right behind me," Jonathan said to his armor bearer, "for the Lord will help us defeat them!" So they climbed up using both hands and feet, and the Philistines fell back as Jonathan and his armor bearer killed them right and left. They killed about twenty men in all, and their bodies were scattered over about half an acre. Suddenly, panic broke out in the Philistine army, both in the camp and in the field, including even the outposts and raiding parties. And just then an earthquake struck, and everyone was terrified. Saul's lookouts in Gibeah saw a strange sight—the vast army of Philistines began to melt away in every direction. — 1 Samuel 14:6, 11-16 (NLT)

While the rest of the Israelite army was shaking in their boots, Jonathan chose to have faith that God truly was who He said He was and attack those who defied the God of Israel. I like to call Jonathan's courageous act *holy mischief.* He was stirring up trouble in the name of the Lord! We spend too much of our energy trying to maintain the status quo and far too little time moving the Kingdom of God offensively forward. Manhood has been sacrificed on the altar of social acceptance. Don't be afraid to be different than the crowd. Most of the time, their inaction is due to fear. Fear is paralyzing. Be willing to act in faith!

One of the most intriguing things about this story is that it was man-initiated, and God wasn't about to miss out on the fun! With most other battles in the Old Testament, God gave instructions to attack, or the leader consulted God to see if they should advance. Not Jonathan. He was indignant about the Philistines mocking his God and about the Israelites lacking the courage to fight. Instead of trying to muster the weary troops, he launched out with his armor bearer by his side and God at his back. Jonathan just got the ball rolling, and God did the rest.

King Saul and his diminishing army were paralyzed by fear. They were focused on protecting themselves instead of taking ground for God. When we become accustomed to the way God has moved in the past or placated by how we believe He'll move in the future, we can actually miss what God is doing today. Staying fresh with God is a daily endeavor. Growing familiar and complacent is a human trait, not a godly trait. And, it will produce human results every time. If we want a fresh move of the Spirit of God, we must pursue His heart constantly.

...No one puts new wine into old wineskins. The new wine would burst the old skins, spilling the wine and ruining the skins. New wine must be put into new wineskins. But no one who drinks the old wine seems to want the fresh and the new. "The old is better," they say. — Luke 5:37-39 (NLT)

Every time I read this scripture, I sigh with disappointment. Many Christians want to drink the old wine rather than go to the trouble of preparing for the new. Old wineskins become rigid and brittle over time. If new wine is placed in them, the fermentation process would burst the fragile skins.

Historically, instead of throwing away the old wineskins, they would be put through a renewal process, resulting in pliable, useable new wineskins. An old wineskin would be soaked in water and then rubbed vigorously with olive oil. Then, it would be ready to handle the new wine being poured in. I think you see the parallel. God pours out His Holy Spirit in fresh, new ways through both intimacy and creativity. The preparation of our hearts and congregations is critical to receiving the new. What causes me to sigh when I read that scripture is the numbers of Christians who won't change to accommodate what God is wanting to do. The only reason we would reject such a washing and renewing experience with the Lord is selfishness. We want what's predictable because we feel we can't control the unknown. The Holy Spirit actually wants us out of control! We need to be on the edge of our seats waiting to see what the Holy Spirit is up to. Instead, most people go on with their lives, expecting Him to walk alongside like a dutiful child. No more! Like Jonathan or Joshua and Caleb, we must walk to the drumbeat of the ever-changing methods of our Leader. Numbers 14:24 (NLT) is my life-verse.

> But my servant Caleb is different from the others. He has remained loyal to me, and I will bring him into the land he explored. His descendants will receive their full share of that land.

The Israelites, after spending over a year outside Egypt, sent twelve spies into the Promised Land to scout out the abundance and the lay of the land. Instead of coming back full of gratitude and faith for what the Lord was about to give them, ten of the twelve reported unconquerable odds and spread fear among the people. However, Joshua and Caleb saw God's plan as good and trusted Him to bring it to pass. No matter the seemingly insurmountable odds, Joshua and Caleb knew the strength of their God and never doubted. That is the cry of my heart. "Lord, give me eyes to see what You're doing and the courage to believe You'll accomplish all You said You would."

This requires daily saturation in His Word. We will easily drift back into seeing from the world's perspective if we aren't constantly renewing our thinking with the Word of the Lord. Our desire must be for Him! He will keep us pliable and useable if we will remain near Him. To think and be led by our own thoughts is to be brittle and unyielding, rejecting the leading of our Savior. To yield ourselves completely to Him and His Word is to show reverence toward Him

Our reverence is based on our concept of how big God is. Do we make Him equal to our size, or do we see Him as He is? If we truly believe that He is severely just, uncompromisingly holy, unimaginably power-ful, incomprehensibly merciful, and amazingly loving, then we won't have any trouble manifesting an attitude of reverence. Our deference and obedience to this awe-some God bears witness of His "bigness" in our lives.

Chapter Seven

A Place of Revelation

"Then Abraham looked up and saw a ram caught by its horns in a bush. So he took the ram and sacrificed it as a burnt offering on the altar in place of his son. Abraham named the place, 'The Lord Will Provide.' This name has now become a proverb: 'On the mountain of the Lord it will be provided.'" — *Genesis 22:13-14 (NLT)*

THE OLD TESTAMENT character, Abraham, has been deemed the father figure of Christianity. Although we look to Christ as our example, Abraham's life provides us much insight. Genesis twenty-two is a challenging chapter in the life of Abraham. Verse one is rather telling, "Later on God tested Abraham's faith and obedience..." It appears that God was testing Abraham's resolve in holding fast to the promises God had given him. Did Abraham truly believe what God had previously told him regarding the future? At the age of ninety-nine, the Lord appeared to Abraham and said,

> ...For you will be the father of many nations. I will give you millions of descendants who will represent many nations. Kings will be among them! I will continue this everlasting covenant between us, generation, after generation. It will continue between me and your offspring forever. And I will always be your God and the God of your descendants after you. Yes, I will give all this land of Canaan to you and to your offspring forever. And I will be their God. — Genesis 17:5b-8 (NLT)

This promise came when Abraham didn't yet have any children. Now, his son, Isaac, was about fourteen years old, and God issued a seemingly outrageous demand.

> Take your son, your only son—yes, Isaac, whom you love so much—and go to the land of Moriah. Sacrifice him there as a burnt offering on one of the mountains, which I will point out to you. — Genesis 22:2 (NLT)

Not only was God challenging Abraham's love by His command to sacrifice Isaac, God was also challenging Abraham's faith in the promise that had been given so many years earlier. Isaac was the son of promise. He was the conduit through which God would carry out everything He had told Abraham.

Had God lied? Did Abraham not hear the promise correctly? All these years, Abraham had looked at Isaac with the hope of fulfillment. Now, God was telling Abraham to kill the embodiment of the dream. Would

Abraham walk in trust even when God's demand seemed to directly oppose His promise? Abraham's response overwhelmingly answers yes!

> The next morning Abraham got up early. He saddled his donkey and took two of his servants with him, along with his son Isaac. Then he chopped wood to build a fire for a burnt offering and set out for the place where God had told him to go. On the third day of the journey, Abraham saw the place in the distance. "Stay here with the donkey," Abraham told the young men. "The boy and I will travel a little farther. We will worship there, and then we will come right back." — Genesis 22:3-5 (NLT)

Abraham chose to believe God's promise in the face of confusing circumstances. In verse five, Abraham emphatically stated, "...and then *we* will come right back." (italics mine) He knew that somehow this child of promise would live, even if God had to perform a miracle and raise Isaac from the dead. When God speaks, He can be trusted.

Several years ago, God began to speak promises to me regarding my future. I humbly received those promises, some being challenging, some pleasurable, and some sobering. Interestingly, over the next few years, my life was flooded with circumstances that constantly challenged my resolve to hold tightly to those promises. The onslaught of events made the promises look like they would never come to pass. Had God lied? Did I hear the promises correctly? Since that time, I have come to understand the principle of promise, testing, and oath. God's promises given are always followed by a time of testing to solidify your faith in God's ability to follow through. Then, after you have endured the testing, He gives His oath, which is an unchangeable seal upon the deliverance of the promise.

The time of testing is so difficult, yet so necessary. If our faith wavers, bitterness begins to entrench itself in our souls. We must make a choice—do we continue to believe what God said despite the lack of evidence, or do we lose our hope and grow in bitterness, essentially calling God unfaithful? Abraham provides us a beautiful example in his unwavering response.

> And Abraham took the knife and lifted it up to kill his son as a sacrifice to the Lord. At that moment the angel of the Lord shouted to him from heaven, "Abraham! Abraham! ...Lay down the knife," the angel said. "Do not hurt the boy in any way, for now I know that you truly fear God. You have not withheld even your beloved son from me." — Genesis 22:10-12 (NLT)

I am truly amazed at how God stretches and challenges us. We want to believe that God exists to make our lives tolerable, and even pleasant. However, He doesn't exist for us; we exist for Him. He draws us, pushes us to our limits, and then rewards our faithfulness and obedience. That description doesn't sound like easy sailing, and it's absolutely not! God's expectations for us include wholehearted trust in His character and unwavering devotion to His Kingdom. Abraham showed both, and so can we. God's answer, then, to Abraham rewarded his faith and obedience.

> Because you have obeyed me and not withheld even your beloved son, *I swear by my own self* that I will

bless you richly. I will multiply your descendants into countless millions, like the stars of the sky and the sand on the seashore. They will conquer their enemies, and through your descendants, all the nations of the earth will be blessed—all because you have obeyed me. — Genesis 22:16-18 (NLT, italics mine)

If you have received promises from God regarding things yet to come, hold onto those promises. It isn't your responsibility to make them come to pass. God will take care of that in His perfect timing. *Your* responsibility is to remain faithful and obedient. God says,

Indeed I have spoken it;

I will also bring it to pass.

I have purposed it;

I will also do it.

— Isaiah 46:11b (NKJV)

In the face of impossibility, hang on to what God has said. Through the times of testing, don't waver. Remain faithful, and don't grow bitter in the waiting. In your steadfastness, God *will* finish what He started in you. When the time of testing is complete, He will seal His promises to you with an oath. No one (except you by your own disobedience) and nothing can keep God from delivering what He has sworn to you. Believe it!

Chapter Eight

A Place of Resolution

"You have stayed at this mountain long enough. It is time to break camp and move on." — Deuteronomy 1:6-7 (NLT)

JUST AS CRITICAL as our ability to determine when God is calling us aside to rest is the ability to know when He's calling us to move on. God is always moving and shifting us, and our resolution to obey His directives determines our destiny. Our will to cooperate with His ebb and flow in our lives catapults us forward, and our stubbornness stalls us out.

The Israelites had remained at the foot of Mount Sinai for over a year. No doubt, they had settled in, found a way to live in a rather unforgiving environment, and become accustomed to their new way of life. But, God never leaves us where we've been. His word to them was an unmistakable release from what had become their new comfort zone.

> When we were at Mount Sinai, the Lord our God said to us, "You have stayed at this mountain long enough. It is time to break camp and move on. Go to the hill country of the Amorites and to all the neighboring regions—the Jordan Valley, the hill country, the western foothills, the Negev, and the coastal plain. Go to the land of the Canaanites and to Lebanon, and all the way to the great Euphrates River. I am giving all this land to you! Go in and occupy it, for it is the land the Lord swore to give to your ancestors Abraham, Isaac, and Jacob, and to all their descendants." — Deuteronomy 1:6-8 (NLT)

At the foot of Mount Sinai, the Israelites had received a spiritual overhaul and necessary guidelines for the future. Their instructions were complete, and it was time to move forward. After God literally spent almost two years hovering over them and speaking to them through Moses, I truly wanted to believe that they would march into the land with confidence and conquer in God's name. But, with that first generation, that's not what happened.

As mentioned in the last chapter, the twelve spies were sent into the Promised Land to have a look around. Ten came back in fear of the people of the land, yet Joshua and Caleb came back ready to believe God for victory. The Israelites listened to the ten spies, embracing their fear and disbelief. Joshua, Caleb, and Moses were not able to dissuade God's children from yielding to fear. As they prepared to stone Joshua and Caleb,

...the glorious presence of the Lord appeared to all the Israelites from above the Tabernacle. And the Lord said to Moses, "How long will these people reject me? Will they never believe me, even after all the miraculous signs I have done among them?... As surely as I live, and as surely as the earth is filled with the Lord's glory, not one of these people will ever enter that land... None of those who have treated me with contempt will enter it." — Numbers 14:10b-11, 21-22, and 23b (NLT)

It's so disappointing that they cowered. It makes me look at my own humanity square in the face and examine my own level of faith.

Really, it comes down to choices. He calls us aside, and we choose to respond. He speaks, and we choose to listen. He restores, and we choose to cooperate. He sends out, and we choose to step forward. At any point, we could choose to stall out, much like a donkey sits and refuses to go any further. And... *that* decision comes with consequences. Jesus said, "If you try to keep your life for yourself, you will lose it. But if you give up your life for me, you will find true life" (Matthew 16:25, NLT). It all comes down to choices. I made a decision to keep saying yes, to keep choosing the next step in faith.

After three years of focused time with Him, hundreds of volunteer hours giving of myself, and writing three (and one-half!) books, it's time to move on. My season of appointed rest has come to an end, and there is much yet ahead. I will not cower. I will not speak doubt. In His name, I will go forward and accomplish all He has so faithfully spoken. *Selah*

www.ingramcontent.com/pod-product-compliance
Lightning Source LLC
Chambersburg PA
CBHW031633040426
42452CB00007B/803